Alive Again

Find Healing in Forgiveness

Sarah K. Howley

Alive Again: Find Healing in Forgiveness

Copyright © 2020 Sarah K. Howley

All rights reserved. No part of this publication may be reproduced, distributed, or transmitted in any form or by any means, including photocopying, recording, or other electronic or mechanical methods, without the prior written permission of the author, except in the case of brief quotations and certain other noncommercial uses permitted by copyright law.

Flaming Dove Press an imprint of
InspiritEncourage LLC
1602 Belle View Blvd #5081
Alexandria, VA 22307
www.inspiritencourage.com

To receive notices of Sarah's upcoming books, sign up at https://www.inspiritencourage.com/book-readers-subscribe

Quantity sales. Special discounts are available on quantity purchases by churches, associations, and others.

For details, contact the publisher at admin@inspiritencourage.com.

ISBN: 978-1-7369071-2-2 (e-book edition)
ISBN: 978-1-7369071-0-8 (paperback edition)
Library of Congress Control Number: 2021910009

All Bible references are from the New International Version (NIV) unless otherwise noted. Scripture taken from the Holy Bible, NEW INTERNATIONAL VERSION®, NIV® Copyright © 1973, 1978, 1984, 2011 by Biblica, Inc.® Used by permission. All rights reserved worldwide.

Cover, illustrations and interior design by: Ashley Santoro

Editor: Jana Spooner

Details in some anecdotes and stories have been changed to protect the identities of the persons involved.

Printed in the United States of America

Dear Believer,

Alive Again takes its name from the story of the Prodigal Son. The young prodigal returns home and the father is so excited to see his son is alive again, having returned to the father and family. However, the son went through many highs and lows before returning, it was not an simple journey. It is not an easy walk to healing, but the Lord will make his presence known to you as He accompanies you on this path. I applaud you for choosing to pick up this book and address open issues in your life. Know that both the Lord and I are cheering you on in for taking up the challenge to release the past and live free from those hurts.

It's important to note that forgiveness is difficult and that healing is a long-term goal. So please be patient with yourself on this journey. This book is biblically based, so when you need a refresher on the verses or accounts from the Bible, take time to stop and read them before going on. Just remember to be patient.

Alive Again is designed to guide you to think biblically about your current struggles and equip you with God's tools to heal from emotional damage. These tools are reliance on Christ for salvation, Scripture as the basis for faith, and recognizing that lasting change is the result of the power of God, the grace of Christ and the indwelling of the Holy Spirit.

You will be richly rewarded for turning to Him in this walk and I pray that he will daily remind you of these rewards, encourage you in releasing the past and spur you on toward freedom in the Holy Spirit.

May His presence be with you always!

Sarah

VI · ALIVE AGAIN

TABLE OF CONTENTS

Introduction	1
Chapter 1 Reconciled Through Forgiveness	5
Chapter 2 Forgiveness Defined	15
Chapter 3 Unable or Unwilling to Forgive	31
Chapter 4 Flags of Hidden Hurt and Unforgiveness	49
Chapter 5 I Still Hurt; I Still Remember	65
Chapter 6 Unlikely Reconciliation	77
Chapter 7 Biblical Reconciliation	89
Acknowledgments	101
Appendix A	103
Appendix B	113
Appendix C	117
About the Author	125
Endnotes	127

VIII · ALIVE AGAIN

INTRODUCTION

He carried off his inheritance before his father had even grown old. He squandered it on high living—squandered all of it. He ends up as a hired hand, feeding slop to pigs and so hungry that he would have gladly eaten the pig food. Finally, he returns home, hoping at most to become his father's servant, maybe tend his father's pigs and eat real food.

Most of us know the story of the prodigal son found in Luke 15. It is interesting that the son is labeled prodigal, for the meaning is like a two-sided coin. Prodigal is both lavish (positive) and it is wastefully extravagant (negative). So, it would seem the father is also prodigal; this father is lavish.

The father lavishly granted the son's desire to receive an early inheritance. And then he watched as the son walked away with little regard for the family left behind. Perhaps the father understood that a forced relationship is no relationship at all and so released his son. Perhaps he remained confident in the teachings of the young man's lifetime and trusted that he would not stray too far. But, like the one hundred sheep and the one who wandered off, here is the one who wandered off. The father likely went to the end of the drive every day, looking for any sign of his son, asking at the city gates if anyone had heard anything of him.

The son finally realized that his father was good and always had been. (I wonder if he really understood how good our Father is?) Upon his return, the son desired only the position of a lowly servant. But this lavish father welcomed him back, forgave his indiscretions, and re-established him as "son." He even threw a lavish feast in his honor!

Like the steadfast father in Luke 15, our heavenly Father is a perfect example of faithfulness. He is faithful even when we are not (2 Tim. 2:13). That is what forgiveness is about. It is about continuing in relationship, being faithful, even when it hurts. He did it first. God continued in relationship with man even after Adam and Eve had sinned. God Himself made clothes for them (Gen. 3:21). Even when He sent them out of the garden, they still had provisions since the land had been planted with fruit and vegetation. By the third day of creation, before people came into the picture, God had prepared what we needed.

But we know the story—man sinned. There were consequences of wrong action and inaction. But God did not cast us away from Him; He merely stuck to His word. Cain and Abel were obviously introduced to God and had a relationship with Him—or at least some knowledge of God. We know from personal experience that the relationship they had was not the same as the intimacy of walking in the garden. There was a lot between man and God that needed resolving.

The resolution was forgiveness. First, in the imperfect sacrifice in the temple, then in the perfect sacrifice on the cross. The final resolution is Jesus. Jesus is the door to restoring the same relationship that Adam and Eve had with God—the relationship of walking in the garden with their best friend every evening.

We took a peek at the story of the prodigal son, concentrating on the father. Like the son, we long to be back in communion with our Father. We long for restoration, resolution, and reconciliation. This is where our journey begins—with our relationship with our heavenly Father. When we start to grasp the lavish forgiveness of our Father, we can begin to turn that forgiveness toward others. Let's take this opportunity to look at the relationship that we have with God, the triune. How is your relationship (and my relationship) with Jesus, with God, and with the Holy Spirit?

CHAPTER 1
RECONCILED THROUGH FORGIVENESS

We have a lavish Father in Heaven! He has forgiven us and welcomes us back, calling us daughters and sons, co-heirs with Christ.

The questions that I have had in recent readings of the parable of the prodigal son are more about the other son, the older son of this lavish father. This brother got angry and said that he had never disobeyed an order. As I read it now again, it strikes me that perhaps this child has based the relationship with his father on acts and not grace.

How many of us remain in the line of those who "do" for God—we do, and we do, and we do. But we haven't stepped into the life and role of child of the Master. In Luke 15:31, the lavish father says, "You are always with me, and everything I have is yours." Clearly, this child has not claimed all that is his. He has not claimed his position.

By the end of the parable, we see two sons in the father's house with two entirely different relationships with the father. I see these representing two conditions that we Christians find ourselves in: belonging yet not realizing and begging yet not accepting.

The older son stayed where he belonged, so to speak. He grew up at home, took care of his responsibilities, worked, and did as he was told. He was the "good" son, and I bet that is how he was as a little boy as well. Dutiful and obedient. There is nothing wrong with dutiful and obedient, as long as it is also an expression of having the same goals and desires as what you are obedient to. Instead, what we see here is discontent in the older brother when the little brother came home, and a big party was thrown. It sounds like the older brother had other desires in his heart. I can imagine that perhaps he wanted to expand the business, maybe grow fruit and not only barley. Maybe he wanted to get some goats in and make natural products for the skin. But he never did these things. He didn't explore the full potential of his relationship with his father. He didn't converse about possibilities and expansion. Then again, maybe he wanted to do something unrelated to the family business—a different dream. But whatever he wanted, it was clear that he didn't get it; he didn't embrace his full position as son.

The younger son had issues as well. He knew he had done some questionable things, hurtful things. So, he thought he would simply return to the man who raised him and beg for a job, any job, however lowly. I can only imagine that his thoughts on the road home were rather dismal. He must have been slinking along, perhaps thinking a lot about himself and all his mistakes. It hadn't even crossed his mind that he could return to a privileged position by his father's side as son. He couldn't accept that what he had done was not who he was. His past actions were not a reflection of the present reality. He hoped for a job and received love instead.

In both cases, these children were embraced yet did not fully understand. They were children yet were not seeking relationship with their father. They did not understand the character behind the figure of father.

He couldn't accept that what he had done was not who he was.

His past actions were not a reflection of the present reality.

We are Children of the Father

Like these sons, we have been welcomed into the arms of God, our Father. We have been forgiven all wrongs and given access to all His goodness. Have we stepped into it? Have we thrown off the mantle of guilt and accepted the warmth of forgiveness? Have we embraced the relationship, or do we labor in the works? Have we set aside our past to embrace our newness in Christ? Have we acknowledged and claimed His love? Acknowledged and claimed His full and unconditional acceptance of us? Because that is what He offers.

> Which of you, if your son asks for bread, will give him a stone? Or if he asks for a fish, will give him a snake? If you, then, though you are evil, know how to give good gifts to your children, how much more will your Father in heaven give good gifts to those who ask him! (Matt. 7:9-11)

Yet, what have we asked? The younger son returned and asked for little but received much. The older son asked nothing but does much. He does much out of obedience, not love. The Father has sought love. In His love, He has forgiven us and returned us to our rightful place as His children. It is for us to embrace Him, His love, and His gifts! Run to the Father!

If you are reading this, you have likely made a decision for Christ. You have accepted Him as your Lord and Savior. You affirm that as the Son of God, He was crucified, died, and was buried. He then rose on the third day, conquering death and sin, defeating the enemy. Once we accept Christ as our Lord and Savior, the reconciliation is complete. It is then up to us to seek Him out as Adam and Eve did in the garden every day. It is up to us to approach Him and know Him. We can ask for our inheritance or ask to expand the business, or whatever the desires of our heart are. We can talk about our doubts and fears—we will surely learn from Him and grow in faith, love, the fruit of the Spirit, and more. He wants this relationship with us.

This lack of fully stepping into and realizing the forgiveness that we have received is repeated in the story of the king who forgave the debtor. Matthew 18:23-35 tells the story of the unmerciful servant who was forgiven much but was unwilling to forgive a little. I think that this man who owed ten thousand bags of gold is like the older brother of the prodigal son—he did not understand what he had been given. The king granted his freedom! Just as the older son was given access to the whole estate.

Yet the servant went out and continued to act as the stilted and stingy old man rather than the lavish king. Have we understood the debt that we have been released from? Have we understood that we owe *nothing*?

Forgiveness is hard. We know that these stories are all about forgiveness: the unmerciful servant and the prodigal son. The king and the father represent God, who has forgiven us all.

Then the servant—that's you and me, by the way—does not forgive others.

I am glad that this story of the unmerciful servant is in the Bible. It shows that God understands the "hard" of forgiveness—the difficulty and the struggle of it. It shows that He knows we have a hard time with it.

Forgiveness is hard. We hurt. We live with physical and emotional scars of what others have done to us. We know that person who hurt us deserves the same back. But, as Christians, we are not permitted that. "It is mine to avenge; I will repay," says the Lord (Deut. 32:35).

Forgiveness, Not Vengeance

We are instructed to forgive, not avenge. How do we turn our anger and hatred into forgiveness? How do we keep from returning the same pain upon our offenders?

We all know this in our heads. But after abuse, adultery, lies, theft, abandonment, manipulation, and so much else . . . how can we forgive? The pain is too much. The anger grows. The disappointment, the after-effects, the judgment. It is just too much.

> Then Peter came to Jesus and asked, "Lord, how many times shall I forgive my brother or sister who sins against me? Up to seven times?" Jesus answered, "I tell you, not seven times, but seventy-seven times." (Matt. 18: 21-22)

There is again an acknowledgment that this is hard; we are to forgive not once or twice but over and over. Our minds work that way; they continue to bring up the offenses of the past over and over until we forgive.

At this point, I want to tell you that forgiveness is obligatory. But that isn't the case. We do have a choice. It is just a choice with consequences. John 20:23 says, "If you forgive anyone's sins, their sins are forgiven; if you do not forgive them, they are not forgiven." Jesus had just promised that the Holy Spirit would come to be with His disciples. They would need God's Spirit to proclaim the message of forgiveness. I choose at the end of my days to be forgiven of all. So, according to John 20:23, I must forgive as well. In the Lord's Prayer, Jesus taught us to ask God to forgive us to the measure that we have forgiven others. So, my head has already concluded that I really have no choice—I must forgive. For me, it *is* an obligation. I suppose you could say it is for selfish reasons because I want to be in good standing at the end of my days. But even with these strong cautions in Scripture, that does not erase the reality that forgiveness is difficult. But praise God, through Jesus, it is possible.

Reflection

1. What do you feel you might still need to "make up" to God? Or others? Do you sense a debt must be paid, or restitution is necessary for something you have done?

2. How much of your life is about relationship with the Lord, and how much is about good works? Is it a good balance? What needs to change to make it more balanced?

3. Are there things (actions, feelings, words) of the past or the present you need to throw off?

4. How do you define forgiveness?

CHAPTER 2
FORGIVENESS DEFINED

Some time ago, a lady I know, an acquaintance from church, shared some difficulties in her marriage. And I felt strongly that a lot was going on behind her words. I said that it sounded like she needed a lot of forgiveness. Her response of "I can't, I just don't think I can" shouldn't have surprised me. But it did.

Why do we say we cannot? As we outlined in the previous chapter, we must forgive to the measure we have been forgiven. Yet, we must also admit that forgiveness is not a simple one-and-done teaching. What I mean is that Jesus returns to this idea of forgiveness numerous times. It is as if He is saying that He understands; He gets that forgiveness is not easy. As in Matthew 18:21-22, Jesus acknowledges that forgiveness is challenging—we are to forgive not seven times, but seventy-seven times.

Let's not get too far ahead without defining forgiveness. I mean, what is it? Is it clearing another person's debt against us? Wiping the slate clean? We all know it is much more complicated than that. If I could wipe the slate clean, then I could forget the offense. But that is not what happens. Ergo, that is not forgiveness.

UC Berkeley Greater Good Science Center states that:

"Psychologists generally define forgiveness as a conscious, deliberate decision to release feelings of resentment or vengeance toward a person or group who has harmed you, regardless of whether they actually deserve your forgiveness."[1]

Wikipedia has a lengthy article on the topic, beginning with:

"Forgiveness . . . is the intentional and voluntary process by which one who may initially feel victimized, undergoes a change in feelings and attitude regarding a given offense, and overcomes negative emotions such as resentment and vengeance (however justified it might be)."[2]

I think that secular theory often has a way of affirming what the Bible says. These two definitions do a decent job of saying something about forgiveness. But the root of forgiveness is in God. How can you release feelings if they are not released to something or someone? If we release, then does that mean the person is free? In the idea of a debt, that is undoubtedly the case. But what about an offense? What are we releasing to? Why choose to change our feelings? How do you change feelings toward a liar, rapist, or murderer? The root of that change is God. Forgiveness makes sense to me only because of God. We release the debt to God, who also changes our feelings about an offense.

I can even imagine an account book loaded with all that a person has done against me, as well as all the associated feelings. Then that account, with the offender's name on the front, is handed over to God. He is the one who will collect the debt. He will avenge the offense.

But I think defining forgiveness is essential. So, I'll do my best here:

> **Forgiveness** is releasing our feelings about an offense and offender to God so that God can heal us of the hurt and injuries sustained in the offense. This healing has a consequential change in our feelings and actions toward the offender (former offender).

At this point, it is important as well to address some related thoughts around forgiveness. There are many things that we have inserted into the idea of forgiveness that need to be clarified.

First, some NOT things:

> Forgiveness is NOT forgetting the offense.
>
> Forgiveness is NOT reconciliation.
>
> Forgiveness does NOT excuse the offense.

Second, the definition of forgiveness does not include any actions or feelings of the offender. The offender does not have to feel remorse or ask for forgiveness. The act of forgiveness is entirely between me (you) and God. The offender doesn't play a part at all. Forgiveness does not heal the offender, nor does it help them change. It is a bit selfish in that it only helps us change and heal.

Third, forgiveness is action, not feeling. Remember that verse about forgiving not seven times but seventy-seven? That is a decision and action to forgive. There is no "I don't feel forgiving" in the stories we have studied. It is a choice—a choice to take steps to make ourselves well.

When I started thinking about forgiveness for my blog, and again for this book, simple pictures kept coming to mind—images that illustrate what unforgiveness and forgiveness do to us. Here are some sketches of what I've imagined:

Forgiveness makes sense to me only because of God, who also changes our feelings about an offense.

Offense

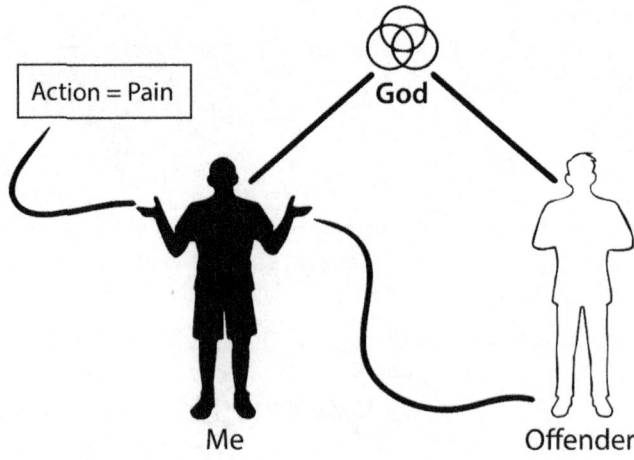

The story begins with an offense, sometimes even multiple offenses during the same incident. Broken trust, broken bones, whispers, lies, yelling, all of it piles on top of us. The offense makes a connection in our minds between that person and pain, between that kind of action and pain.

Unforgiveness Part 1

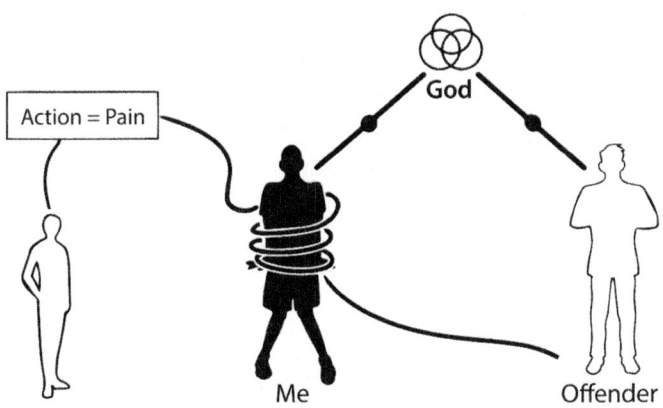

When we don't forgive the offender, that rope seems to grow in our hands and wraps around us like a python, trying to cut off our breath. The pain intensifies when we interact with that person, but it also begins to influence other interactions. Other people may do something that appears similar to the original offense, and the rope tightens its grip and interferes with other relationships. Let's call this the ripple effect. The offense(s) may impact other areas of our lives or relationships that also require our attention as a link or ripple is established. Notice too that the rope doesn't touch the offender. They are not aware of the unforgiveness, and it does not squeeze them in the same way it squeezes us; they go on about life with ease.

There is also now a knot in the relationship you have with the triune God. Unforgiveness will make communion more difficult. There is also a knot on the offender's rope; God will take care of that in due time.

Unforgiveness Part 2

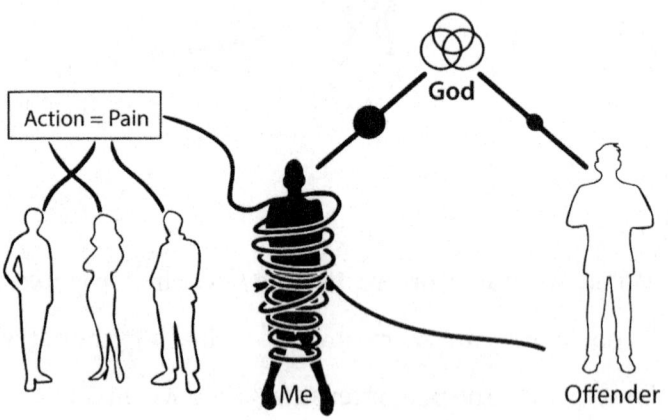

Over time the rope ties itself more and more around us. The pain and the actions of others are more often interfering with our normal functioning as a mature adult. This rope of pain and offense does nothing to the offender. Do you see how the rope doesn't even touch them? But it consumes you. When invited to a party, your first thought may be, "I wonder if so-and-so will be there." And then when you find that they will be, you decide not to go. They hold control and power over you, even without touching the rope of pain and offense. This offense has begun to restrict your actions. And just look how thin you have become because the rope keeps pulling and pulling. Notice too that the communion line with God has gotten shorter, and there is more interference on the line. At this point, we are in continued disobedience, which makes it a very strained relationship. The ongoing ripple effect means the actions of others may begin to inflict unintended pain because they remind you of the first offense. This pain and the actions you take as a result may also inflict pain on others (not attending a party just because the offender is), and a cycle of hurt perpetuates, creating more ripples.

Forgiveness Part 1

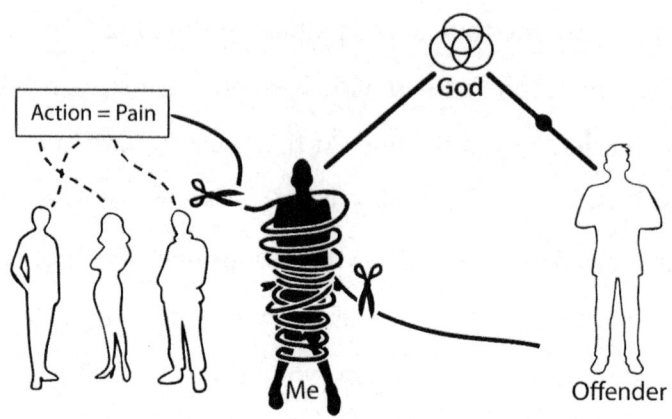

This pattern will continue until you decide on forgiveness. The number of others affected by your moods and even the number of activities you participate in will all change due to your lack of forgiveness.

Once we decide to forgive, once we act out forgiveness, we will feel release from the offender and from the pain and repeated effects on others. This will start with a simple statement of "I forgive so-and-so for X." You don't have to tell that person; it is just between you and God. You may also have to go through a similar process of forgiveness with the other people who have inadvertently hurt you through actions similar to the original offense—the ripple effect. Others will notice the difference in you and wonder at the freedom you have found, and you will too. You may also do some apologizing to people who have been affected by the choices made during the period of unforgiveness. But the real blessing that comes is that you will have re-established communion with our Lord and again feel His indescribable peace.

Forgiveness Part 2

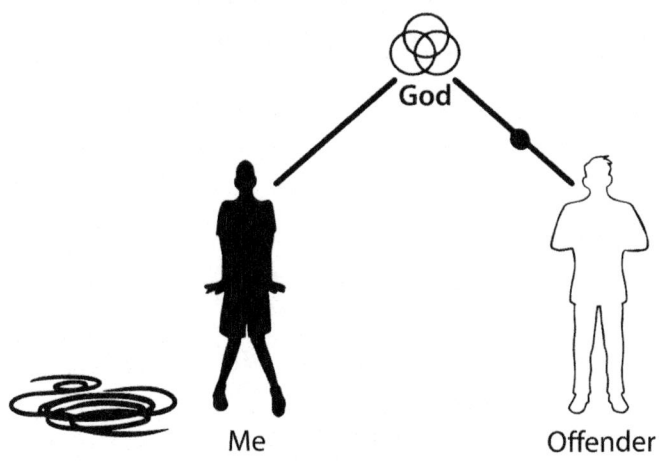

Forgiveness, particularly the "seventy-seven times" kind, will take some time to unwind the rope and allow full forgiveness. When I say full forgiveness, it is an attempt to acknowledge that rarely is forgiveness required for a single "act." And even if it is a single "act," that act likely has varied facets of associated pain. An example of a single act with varied facets is being stood up for coffee with a friend. The associated pain may be from rejection as well as loneliness or anxiety. So, as these different facets of the single act are addressed, forgiveness is more fully realized.

When the offense and the pain come to mind and heart, again and again, it is vital to repeat forgiveness statements. The rope *will* drop off. There may be a few hitches here or there, and the rope tries to come back around you, but through persistence, it won't. The offender is still responsible for their actions to God; that is why there is still a knot there. God and the offender will handle that. In faith, we accept that God will handle that. But there is no longer a tie to the offender or the offense.

Forgiveness Part 3

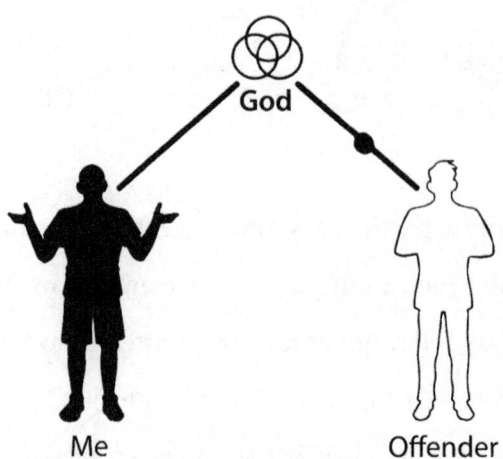

In a short time, you will be in full communion with God again and undertaking His work in new and wonderful ways.

You will no longer be squeezed or take that sharp inhale when someone does something *seemingly* similar to the hurt inflicted by the offender. The lack of forgiveness is what kept you tied up to the offender. You will be healed. The offense and the offender are in God's hands. The offender has to deal with their issues, and we have to deal with ours.

So far as it is in my control to obey God, I want to. I want to forgive. It isn't a feeling; forgiveness is a choice, an action.

Reflection

1. Take a moment to consider the offenders in your life. Who have you forgiven? Who have you been unable to forgive?

2. Ask God in prayer to open your eyes to those you may not have forgiven and those to whom you may need to repent.

3. What is your definition of forgiveness now? How has your definition changed over time, from a child to now?

4. Are you ready to move forward unfettered?

CHAPTER 3
UNABLE OR UNWILLING TO FORGIVE

"I just can't forgive him for that." Or maybe you are thinking, "I just can't forgive her for that. It hurt too much. What am I going to do?" It is a struggle to forgive immediately, despite what we know we *should* do.

We have all heard stories like Mary Johnson's. In 1993, her son was murdered by her next-door neighbor. But she forgave him. Eventually, it came:

> Mary gives God the glory with her ability to forgive such a tragedy, 'unforgiveness is like cancer. It will eat you from the inside out. It's not about the other person, me forgiving him does not diminish what he's done. Yes, he murdered my son—but the forgiveness is for me. It's just for me.'[3]

We struggle a ton with forgiveness, and it seems to fall into three categories—three reasons we say we cannot forgive. One is that we think forgiveness should be earned. The second is that we think not forgiving the person will hurt *them*. The third is that we believe God is too merciful to carry out justice (we don't trust Him). We'll look at each of these separately.

Forgiveness Earned

The first—that forgiveness must be earned in order for us to give it—is a common desire. This thought relates closely to repentance. We feel repentance should precede forgiveness. We could look again at the parable of the prodigal son for examples of how the father accepted the sons, forgiving them and not expecting anything in return. But I think there is a better illustration.

Jesus was treated horribly on His way to the cross. What did the soldiers deserve? They have beaten Him, flogged Him, made Him carry the heavy burden of the cross, stolen His clothes, and nailed Him naked to the cross. Have they earned His forgiveness? Have they even asked for forgiveness? Absolutely not! Yet, Jesus said, "Father, forgive them, for they do not know what they are doing" (Luke 23:34). There was no repentance by the soldiers, but forgiveness was certainly given.

So, that is a good example, but after all, we are talking about Jesus here. He is a bit better at this than we are! But Scripture gives us other examples. Consider Joseph and his brothers. He, too, was severely mistreated, but he did indeed forgive them. Then there are the brothers Esau and Jacob. Let's look at this story to dispel any lingering doubts about our ability to forgive. In Genesis 25:29-34, Esau sold Jacob his birthright for the price of a bowl of lentil stew and some bread. And two chapters later, Jacob stole the blessing of their father as well. Jacob fled by the end of the chapter, knowing that his brother was out to get him now. Jacob then spent many years working for his uncle, earning the right to marry his daughters and to have flocks to take as his wages. It is estimated to be over twenty years before Jacob was ready to return to his family with his wives. As he headed back, he sent messengers ahead and hoped for good. But he planned for the worst. He basically thought about bribing his brother to let him come home, waylaying him with gifts as he approached. In Genesis 33:4, the scene of the reunion is quite touching: "But Esau ran to meet Jacob and embraced him; he threw his arms around his neck and kissed him. And they wept." Esau forgave without expecting anything from his brother. We hear little of Esau after this, but he is an excellent example of the forgiveness that is possible.

There are also the times that Jesus taught on forgiveness and other passages in the New Testament that speak of forgiveness. The only condition mentioned in the various passages is that we will be forgiven in the measure we forgive (Matt. 6:14-15). We cannot neglect Luke 17:3-4 that says, "If your brother or sister sins against you, rebuke them; and if they repent, forgive them. Even if they sin against you seven times in a day and seven times come back to you saying 'I repent,' you must forgive them." So, we must be quick to forgive when others are repentant, but there is no teaching that says we *only* forgive when or if they repent. This would be earning forgiveness. And we know that we ourselves are very undeserving of the forgiveness we have received.

Just how would we intend to earn the forgiveness of God? If forgiveness could be earned here on earth, why not hold us to the same standard with God? Thankfully, we have these examples in Scripture, and we know there is nothing we can do or even feel about forgiveness to earn it. In turn, we certainly cannot expect others to earn it. Forgiveness is truly grace at its most basic form.

Unforgiveness as Punishment to Others

We feel justified in our hurt, and more than likely, we *are* just in hurting. It is important to permit ourselves to feel how we feel and process through those emotions. I lived for too long with the thought that I had to simply contain emotions and not actually understand what I was feeling and how to process them. Hurt is one of those emotions and should be explored. What hurts and why? But let's face it—no one wants to remain in pain.

Emotional pain can linger for entirely too long, especially due to withholding our forgiveness. Our thought may be, "I am still hurting, and they should too," or, "I don't want to let them off the hook for the offense as long as I am still hurting." The truth of forgiveness is that withholding it only hurts *us*. The anger and hurt over the offense set down roots; the root of bitterness grows from unforgiveness.

The lack of forgiveness also deepens the pain and anger we feel. The lack of forgiveness means that we have open wounds as we walk around and carry out our everyday affairs. Those open wounds are easily scratched and pushed upon, broadened, and deepened by others and the original offender. By not forgiving, we leave ourselves open for deeper wounding.

Withholding forgiveness as a punishment also assumes that the person is aware of the offense. I suspect that many are not thinking of the harm they have done to us; they are going along, living their lives, feeling justified in *their* actions and feelings. The offender is only interested in knowing if we have forgiven them if they are repentant. Just above, we noted that repentance is not a requirement of forgiveness. The whole argument really just falls apart at this point. They are likely unaware or uncaring and therefore not hurting because of our withholding forgiveness—all while we hurt ourselves, and we grow bitter. It all impacts us badly and the offender not at all.

If we consider popular movies and books, we have several examples of why this doesn't work out quite the way we expect. In *A Christmas Carol*, we have Scrooge, who has been miserly and miserable to others for years; but he has no idea that is who he has become. It takes a significant shake-up for him to see it.

He, as the offender, is unaware of the offense. Withholding forgiveness wouldn't affect him at all.

Then we have the movie *Liar Liar*; do you remember the one with Jim Carrey as a lawyer? The main character, Fletcher Reede, doesn't view his offense the way others do. His lying hurts his son every single time, and he just doesn't process lying as we, or God, would want him to. Again, it takes a drastic 24-hour experience to change the man. He simply didn't care, or maybe care enough, that he hurt his son. Withholding forgiveness wasn't an impact for him either.

The last example is *The Devil Wears Prada*, where the boss Miranda (Meryl Streep) doesn't consider anyone's needs or feelings throughout the whole film. She insults and belittles constantly. I flinched through the entire film whenever Miranda opened her mouth, hoping for a change of heart. In the end, there was no change because the young staff member Andy, played by Anne Hathaway, recognizes that she cannot influence the boss at all and quits the job. Throughout the entire film, the offender never realizes the horror and outrage that she inflicts on others. Withholding forgiveness doesn't touch Miranda at all.

We stubbornly want that other person to change, but all along, we are incapable of inflicting change on the offender. It is in our own humbling and re-prioritization that healing comes. It is a personal reckoning, led by the Holy Spirit, that brings about our change of heart.

And sometimes, the offender does change. Scrooge comes to understand who he has become, and Fletcher recognizes that family is more important than work. But when no change comes, we still must choose healing—Andy decides to release her hurt instead of suffering, which brings a change in her. In two of these stories, the changes come following supernatural intervention. But in every case, the offender only changes when they choose, not when we choose.

We walk in our own stubborn way, thinking that we can inflict hurt on others by not forgiving. The stubborn way of Christ, though, is to forgive. Every single time. Forgiveness is not a "feeling." Feeling like forgiving someone isn't biblical. Forgiveness is a choice. And it is a "many times" thing. A seventy-seven times thing (Matt. 18:21-22). So, in obedience, we just have to start with the words, and the Spirit will lead the rest of the way. Each time the hurt and the offense come to mind, even seventy-seven times, we just have to say, "I forgive, Lord—help me forgive because I want to heal."

Lack of Trust in God

The third reason we have difficulty releasing our hurt and pain for God to deal with is that we have difficulty trusting He will punish the offender. We seek vengeance on the offender, whether through passive or active means, and we want God to be very active in His punishment. But as Christians, we know God as Father and forgiver, as He who sacrificed His own son to reconcile us to Him. And to reconcile the offender. So, we, perhaps understandably, think that God will not punish the offender. We have never seen such happen (and we have probably prayed for it to happen!), and we suspect that God will be merciful rather than vengeful.

Forgiveness does not release the offender of accountability for their actions. Forgiveness has nothing to do with the offender but has everything to do with choosing our own healing and choosing ourselves over the offender. The offender is *not* released from the offense; we are released from the pain.

Recall the definition of forgiveness that we proposed in chapter two. Here it is again: Forgiveness is releasing our feelings about an offense and offender to God so that God can heal us of the hurt and injuries sustained in the offense.

But we don't just want release; we want vengeance. Maybe the definition needs to say that too? We release our desire for vengeance to God as part of forgiveness. Should we say it this way instead? Forgiveness is releasing our feelings about (and desire for revenge for) an offense and offender to God so that God can heal us of the hurt and injuries sustained in the offense.

Honestly, it comes back to faith. We believe in Christ as Lord and Savior; we have professed our faith in Him and call ourselves "Christian" or "believer." We believe in the promise that we have in that faith: that we will be with Him in heaven and have everlasting life. But we don't believe in this promise of the Lord: "It is mine to avenge; I will repay" (Deut. 32:35). Why don't we step back and let Him save us from the hurt? He can save us from the hurt and pain in faith. So, in the midst of this struggle, we must hold on to this: He is the only one that can carry out revenge. And He will. This very same verse continues, "It is mine to avenge; I will repay. In due time their foot will slip; their day of disaster is near and their doom rushes upon them."

Perhaps we struggle to believe that God will act and act swiftly because we are surrounded by a world that seems to thrive on evil, and no punishment is in sight. Everywhere we turn, we find lies, deceit, murder, bribery, fraud, theft, trolling, human trafficking, bribery, extortion. And we ask a resounding "Where is God in this? Where is He in my pain?" Faith. Faith is the only answer I can give for this. We stand on faith. We stand firm upon the rock of our *faithful* God. God is good. Faith. We believe so many other things about our God, we need to just cry out, "Help my unbelief, Lord!" (See Mark 9:24)

The offender is still accountable to God for that offense, but how or when God holds them accountable is not our concern. Faith. God will hold them to it. "But I tell you that everyone will have to give account on the day of judgment for every empty word they have spoken. For by your words you will be acquitted, and by your words you will be condemned" (Matt. 12:36-37). We will all give an account. Our unforgiveness will also be held to account (ouch!).

The offender is not released from the offense; we are released from the pain.

From Can't to Forgiveness

At this point, perhaps you are leaning toward forgiveness, however reluctantly it may be. The simple declarations, like "I forgive" and "Help my unbelief," will make a difference in your heart. These simple statements and the outpouring of pain in prayer to God will release the control that pain and hurt have in our lives. The lack of forgiveness and the desire for revenge have wrapped us up so tightly, we are broken people. But the release to God will change us and make us more like Jesus.

Forgiveness opens us up to the Lord and His desires for our good. The string that tied us to the offender is broken, and their actions no longer dictate our own. Did you always leave the party when the offender arrived? No longer—because God gives back what you lost. Did you use to respond rashly to demands? No longer—your blood doesn't boil, and you don't lose all reason; you calmly reply that you have other priorities, and you will let them know when it can be completed.

God wants us to be healthy and whole. Forgiveness is one of the tools that He implores us to use to achieve that state. Let us forgive as He has forgiven.

A Note on Bitterness

Most of us know King Saul in the Bible. He was the first

king of Israel, chosen by God, and described as handsome and a head taller than anyone else (1 Sam. 9:2). I haven't spent much time considering Saul. I admit that I generally skip to David.

But in looking into biblical references to bitterness and unforgiveness, Saul was clearly a bitter man in regard to David.

What was David's offense? He stole the hearts and admiration of the people. And Saul's heart grew bitter. He didn't do anything to counter the loss, nor did he change his perspective into one where he was proud of David and the nation's accomplishments. There is no evidence of forgiveness either. Instead, he began to attack David. By the time David arrived in Saul's life, Saul had already turned away from God. He hid at his own coronation, he disregarded God's will, he repeatedly chose not to seek God's will before battle and didn't seek God at the very battle where David established his abilities against Goliath. His bitterness grew into actually seeking the death of David, hunting him with scouts and armies.

Another example of bitterness comes from Ruth. I always had kind of skipped over this woman who goes from being called Naomi to Mara, from sweetness to bitterness. Ruth 1:20-21 says:

> "Don't call me Naomi," she told them. "Call me Mara, because the Almighty has made my life very bitter. I went away full, but the Lord has brought me back empty. Why call me Naomi? The Lord has afflicted me; the Almighty has brought misfortune upon me."

So, here we have bitterness, and wow, I think most of us would say that she has lost everything, and it is not a surprise that she is so negative. But I don't see forgiveness or unforgiveness, only loss—severe loss. So often, this is the point of sermons on bitterness: that its root is unforgiveness. Usually, we turn to Hebrews 12:15 to discuss this, which says, "See to it that no one falls short of the grace of God and that no bitter root grows up to cause trouble and defile many." But there is another verse that also mentions the words root and bitterness: Deuteronomy 29:18. This verse says, "Make sure there is no man or woman, clan or tribe among you today whose heart turns away from the Lord our God to go and worship the gods of those nations; make sure there is no root among you that produces such bitter poison." The connection of turning away from God and producing bitter poison is unmistakable. It is the turning away from God that causes bitterness.

Consider our dear King Saul again. Even before he met David, he had forsaken God. And with each of David's victories, Saul's bitterness grew. Then consider Naomi/Mara. She blamed God for her losses; she did not turn to Him for comfort but turned away from Him in anger and pain. It seems too that Naomi lost trust in God, trust that He would turn all things for good for those who love Him (Rom. 8:28). Or the Old Testament equivalent, that what enemies intend for bad God can turn for good (Gen. 50:20). We, just like Mara, also turn away from Him in our anger. Like King Saul, we do not trust, do not wait, do not seek God, and our hearts grow bitter. We do not seek Him in our pain and anger. We do not trust that He will do as He says. And bitterness takes root.

Reflection

1. Take a moment to consider those who have wronged you. Are you waiting for anyone to deserve forgiveness? Are there any that you are waiting on to ask forgiveness from you or be repentant? Pray for God to work in your heart to forgive them. Even say that you do.

2. Is there anyone you have thought of punishing or hurting by not forgiving them? Pray for release of these desires.

3. Do you trust God to justly deal with the offender's sin? Pray for God to increase your faith so you can release your hurts to Him.

4. Are you ready to forgive? If you need time, don't continue immediately to the next chapter. Instead, take time in prayer and reflection. Pray that God will soften your heart and prepare you to move on from the hurt.

5. On bitterness: Are you turning away from God or seeking Him every day? And how about more specifically in the struggle to forgive? Seeking Him will keep you from growing that bitter root and will pull up any that may have begun over time.

CHAPTER 4
FLAGS OF HIDDEN HURT AND UNFORGIVENESS

Have you ever overreacted to something and wondered why? Or have others told you that you shouldn't have acted that way? These are signs that something is hiding under those actions. An old pain is there and festering. This is part of the brokenness we carry around with us. It might be related to old unforgiveness. We could say these are the ripples of the hurt that we have experienced.

Let's consider an example of someone who was abused as a child. In this example, the unresolved issues may come out in future intimate relationships, or when that person's children get to be the same age as they were when abused. These ripples can be the consequence of a single act or multiple acts that may seem unrelated. But the past "act" also influences present circumstances.

Flag: Inappropriate Reaction

When I sang in the church choir several years ago, we began a new season, and at one of the first rehearsals, it was announced that we would be meeting an hour later than we had previously. I lived in a large city without a car and was at the mercy of public transportation. Starting rehearsal an hour later made me want to quit right then and there. I was irate and couldn't understand why there had been no consultation. I felt like the "privileged" people who owned a car or motorbike wouldn't have a problem because any location in town was only twenty minutes away at that time of night. But I had to go an hour by public transport, alone, waiting and walking at night in the dark. I was livid and felt like no one cared about me just because of a change in the hour of rehearsal. Can you hear how upset I was?

I can look back on it now and see that I overreacted. I was irrational. At the time, I was blessed to have people watching over me who noted my reaction and asked me to think about it. I agreed to talk it out with a trusted church member.

In talking it through, it didn't take long to identify that when I was a youth, I felt like I was left out and not good enough. This feeling was reinforced over time through small but many incidents. In talking about it, I realized that one person was repeatedly involved in those incidents. It took looking at the underlying emotions to understand that I was hurt by the choir director in the present, yes, but that I was also hurt in my past, and this past hurt was influencing my present.

Forgiving both—the present offender and the past hurt—was necessary for me to move forward. Every time those feelings of inadequacy and unimportance came up again, I had to call them out and remind myself the offense was forgiven. No matter the actions of others, I am capable and important, as God has created me to be. This was not an overnight thing—it was an over time thing. In time, God took those feelings inflicted by others and erased them. Forgiveness led to changes in me, in my relationships, and in my responses to slights.

Sometimes pain and hurt are slapping us in the face, and we know exactly what happened and who we need to forgive. But sometimes, we need to understand ourselves better. Sometimes we have to understand the ripple effect is showing up in our reactions, and we have to ask God to work in us to heal the seemingly unrelated issues. It is a process. We need to seek Him and, when we do, the things that He wants to change in us will become obvious. We have to be willing to consider our actions and reactions in order to notice when we are being irrational or otherwise responding to unrelated hurt—the hurt under there that we have not yet dealt with.

Flag: Uncharacteristic Reaction

Over the past few months, I noticed that a gal I knew in high school, who attended the same church youth group as me, was posting on Facebook about a recent loss. As these posts have gone on, I have thought about her several times and was thinking about her again just this week. I was praying for her, asking for God to console her. And I asked myself why I hadn't put a message of condolence on her Facebook page. I felt put off by contacting her, even by leaving a simple message on Facebook. I couldn't help but think that was odd. I am usually the one who follows up and asks after others or notices when something is off. I usually reach out. Why didn't I want to reach out to her?

It has indeed been years since we knew each other, but clearly, I felt something in her pain. While praying and talking to God, I realized that I had a bit of animosity toward her. And that was when God revealed that I felt that way because I was rejected by the group as a youth. I had already processed and forgiven the leaders of the group, as well as my brother, who had made decisions I didn't agree with. I really felt like I was done with the work of forgiving in this situation and that I had "fully forgiven." But I hadn't ever turned my thoughts or forgiveness toward the other individuals in the group. In fact, I passed it off as "they were young and didn't know what they were doing . . . oh how sad." These were the very words of Jesus from the cross.

"Father, forgive them, for they do not know what they are doing" (Luke 23:34). But the reality is that they did hurt me, and it took thirty years to forgive them. I held on to the hurt of the "act" for a long time, not knowing what to do with it. Some of it God had dealt with through counseling about fifteen years ago. But there was still something hanging on. So, I released it. I actually felt something inside me let go when I forgave them. Little pictures of them all floated through my head, and I whispered, "I forgive you," and a tightness eased in me.

I never even interacted with anyone else in the case I described above, but I still noticed an inconsistency in my reaction. God can use those reflective moments when we know something is off to bring us back to Him. He brings us back closer to Him when we forgive. The distance that time brings may also filter out what still needs His balm. I have no current link to this woman or many people from that period of my life and even shied away from them a bit. Now I understand why and feel no need to do so anymore. Another of the group was recently married, and I now feel free to say congratulations. Part of me wants to say this was a ripple effect. Many in the group never intended harm, as their actions were consequences of other's actions. But it still required me to let go and forgive.

Even the hurts that were inadvertent are deeply felt. And I can't expect any one of these folks to come to me and ask forgiveness. They don't know what impact their actions and inactions made on my life. Beth Moore, in her book *Chasing Vines*, says something similar about forgiveness. She says, "I've become increasingly convinced that those we need to forgive most often grasp the least how much they've hurt us. If they understood and took responsibility, it wouldn't have taken the cross to forgive them. It could have just happened over coffee."[4] I would go so far as to say no one that we need to forgive understands the depth of our pain or the impact they had on our inner lives. Beth Moore makes the important point: forgiveness required the cross. It takes the cross for me to understand and grasp forgiveness—to grasp the depth of what I've been forgiven, as the unmerciful servant in Matthew 18 did not. I need not carry my mistakes, my sin, and my hurt around with me. I have been truly set free, am alive again; and that has happened through the forgiveness that I received because of the cross. As I extend that same forgiveness, I am set free and set others free.

I need not carry my mistakes, my sin, and my hurt around with me.

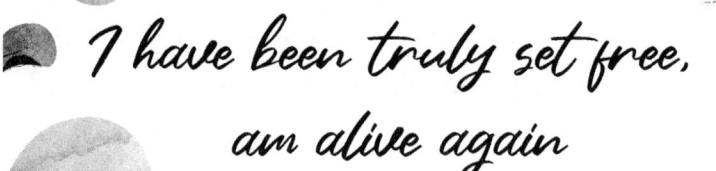

I have been truly set free, am alive again

Flag: Regret of the Past

We have looked at how our actions and reactions may indicate that we have some unresolved forgiveness and pain to deal with. God also uses regret to gently remind us to turn to Him for forgiveness and healing. Are there people you shy away from because you wronged them, or maybe they were witnesses to your tantrum, like mine above? The regret of our own actions in response to hurt and unforgiveness can make us either turn inward or turn to God.

I don't know what made David sleep with a married woman and then have her husband killed. As a man after God's own heart, we expect a bit more out of him, don't we? But I think that is why we like David so much. Much like Peter denying Jesus three times, David made mistake after mistake and still was called a man after God's own heart. It gives us hope for all the mistakes we have made and that our relationship with God can be close too.

I have always thought the story of David and Bathsheba was a bit odd. We tend to focus on David's adultery and not Bathsheba's. I wonder when she began to regret her adultery. Was it only when she learned that she was pregnant? How did she fall under David's spell with such apparent ease? The Bible doesn't tell us of a struggle within her, but there didn't seem to be much time in the wooing. David didn't have to court her much before she fell into his arms. Yet her husband was an upstanding man who thought of his fellow soldiers and didn't want to enjoy his home life when they could not. This implies that Bathsheba had a decent husband (nothing like the man that David's second wife Abigail married—Nabal, the "fool").

We know nothing of Bathsheba other than she was a beautiful woman who turned a king's head. Perhaps her own head was empty. Maybe not since she gave birth to the wise Solomon. Maybe she felt the power of the king as opposed to a real decision to betray her vows. We know that Bathsheba was to be found out, and others would talk—pregnancy does that. We learn of her regret when she sent word to David and made it his problem. The unfortunate thing was that she seemed to miss the opportunity to deal with her bad decision; the wrongdoing didn't seem to make a difference to her. Bathsheba didn't take notice of the regret as a way to turn to God. She turned to man to take care of this problem.

Response to Regret

David also looked to an earthly solution to the problem. He tried to get the husband home to sleep with his wife. David even got him drunk, and still, the man wouldn't go home. So, David had the man carry his own death sentence to the battlefield. And Uriah, Bathsheba's husband, was killed in battle. Where did the man after God's own heart disappear to? David did not turn to God at the adultery. Nor at the pregnancy. Nor at the deception of the husband, twice over. Nor did he call out to God before taking the man's life.

One mistake led to another and another and another. May I be so bold as to say: one sin led to another and another and another sin.

Bathsheba experienced regret when she knew her sin would be made public; her pregnancy was a blaring sign of wrongdoing. David didn't seem to express this. He wanted to cover his mistake, which would also cover hers. I think we experience regret so that we can correct what we have done, but here we have a classic example of man's correction and not God's.

Regrets Should Turn Us to God

It takes the prophet Nathan telling an allegory before David saw his own sin. The regret that David expressed is not only sorrow for the act itself, but he said, "I have sinned against the Lord" (2 Sam. 12:13). The regret has everything to do with the actions being *against God*. Many of us experience regret of the past, but it is what we do with it that makes the difference. David *finally* took it to God. In the very same verse, we read, "The Lord has taken away your sin." It takes God no time to ponder; He removes the blot immediately, in the same verse, the same breath, so to speak. Instant forgiveness.

David must have carried this around for a good long while since the child had already been born; months have gone by with this sin festering. But the *moment* that David acknowledged the sinful situation, it was forgiven. Having turned to God instead of his own strength, he was absolved of the sin and restored to God.

David worshiped God. That was the next thing he did. He learned that his child had died, and he cleaned up and went to worship God. The Lord gives, and the Lord takes away. He is still worthy to be praised.

David washed, worshiped, and ate. He took care of what was necessary, and worship is necessary. Worship takes us to the place that David came to: the realization that we cannot change the consequences by acting out or lamenting the loss. David accepted the loss and comforted his wife. I can't say, "and he went on with life." After all, the point of regret is to get us to change what we were doing. I have to say I would prefer if the Bible said that Bathsheba forgave as well, as there is still someone and some action left out here. The adultery (or rape as some posit) and death of her husband would have warranted some serious consideration and time for forgiveness, in my view.

Change of Heart

Another example of someone who must have experienced regret is the adulteress in the New Testament that Jesus comes upon just before she is stoned to death. This again highlights that the point of regret is to sin no more. Jesus said, "Then neither do I condemn you . . . go now and leave your life of sin" (John 8:11). The adulteress encountered Jesus and had a change of heart. David also acknowledged to the Lord that he had sinned and had a change of heart. God wants us to change our behavior, but that requires His intervention in the heart. That change of heart then leads to altered behavior.

These examples show us firstly that sin against one another is ultimately a sin against God and secondly that we have the choice of going before God to ask for that forgiveness. God corrects and changes our hearts so we become more like Him. But He can only do that when we meet Him, go to Him. Then as we return to His side and are no longer separated from God by that sin, we can walk in His ways. We can walk upright to face the consequences and the fallout of our past.

Not all actions that we regret and confess to God have such dire consequences, nor are they usually so linear. In David's case, sin's consequence was that the child died. Often, our sin or pain and forgiveness stories have knock-on effects and things that we have to deal with over time. The relationships change, the expectations of others change. But in having sought forgiveness through Christ's redemptive action on the cross, we are no longer alone to deal with them, for Christ walks with us.

Forgiving Ourselves

I think when we consider David—and particularly this incident—he must have also dealt with the personal repercussions of his choices. There are things that we have done that we regret and want to kick ourselves over. But what we are called to do is this: "If we confess our sins, he is faithful and just and will forgive us our sins and purify us from all unrighteousness" (1 John 1:9). The confession of sins begins the road to forgiving ourselves. And the results are the same as when we forgive others. When we forgive others, we release our feelings about an offense and offender to God so that God can heal us of the hurt and injuries sustained in the offense. This healing produces a consequential change in our feelings and actions toward the offender. The same thing happens when we forgive ourselves. God wants to heal us of the injuries both to others and ourselves in the offense, and this healing will change our actions and feelings. Forgiving ourselves means no longer berating ourselves for our mistakes; rather, it entails accepting responsibility for our mistakes and the pain we have caused others. It means growing in Christ, so we don't make that mistake again. David showed us in this incident that these things can take time. Using David as a model, we can do as he did in forgiving ourselves. We can ask God for forgiveness, forgive ourselves, address the issue with those we hurt, empathize with them, and take the opportunity to grow in Christ and change our hearts. Many of the topics in the next chapter can help us in this journey.

Reflection

1. Are there times that come to mind when you have had an inappropriate reaction? Pray for understanding of the issue so it can be resolved.

2. Have others noted an uncharacteristic reaction in you? Have you noticed this in yourself? Take time to note these instances and prayerfully consider the reasons behind your reaction.

3. Consider listing regrets you carry around and addressing them as David did.

CHAPTER 5
I STILL HURT; I STILL REMEMBER

While the step of forgiveness is a choice, a seemingly brief action, the healing takes time. Healing following forgiveness is actually a ton of work. Some forgiveness requires little work, like the person I don't know who let the door slam in my face when my hands were full. I forgive them and go on with no rancor. However, when we turn to the long-term friendships and family relationships that we have, those take more work. It took a ton of work to get us here in the first place, and it'll take a ton of work to get us out of the pain we are in.

In Mark 10:46-52, we find the story of blind Bartimaeus. Bartimaeus was calling out to Jesus, who gathered him close and asked what he wanted from Jesus. We expect the answer; we expect Bartimaeus to ask to see. Jesus knows Bartimaeus better than we do, so He likely saw beyond the blindness. He saw all of Bartimaeus' hurts. The scars and burns, the bruises, the heart hurts, and the bitterness. He sees all of our hurts and wants to take care of all of us. But He waits for an invitation. He waits to address each hurt for the time when we are ready.

We may have a lot of hurts from long-term relationships. We may have just one. But the pain is huge either way. Forgiveness is the release and healing of ourselves for the hurt inflicted.

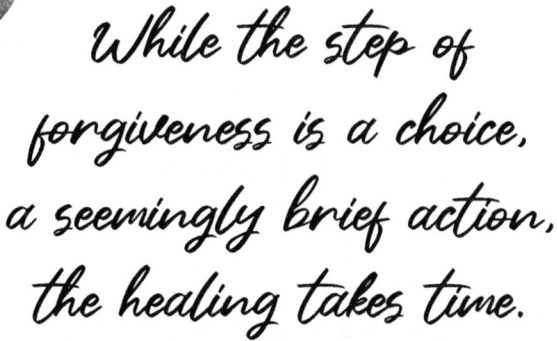

While the step of forgiveness is a choice, a seemingly brief action, the healing takes time.

A generic bandage of saying "I forgive you" will help; it will start the healing. But it is like going to an optician when you need an ophthalmologist. Our forgiveness needs to be specific. We need specific surgical intervention into the hurt of our hearts.

The hurt we experience likely affects us in many ways. The people who hurt us often hurt us over and over, and rarely is it only one single act or hurt. There are multiple things to forgive. Sigh. Like a car accident, the crushed bumper leads to a busted radiator, and there is the wheel and the axel and . . . and . . . and. One thing touches another. The ripples of one action impact other aspects of life.

Healing from Hurt

The power of Jesus has been sent to live within us. The power of Jesus' healing resides in the Holy Spirit, in us. The balm and healing occur when we open those areas to God and reveal the hurts, specifically. How do we do that? I want to give you some ideas below to help you get started.

Talk it Out: Revealing hurts of long-term pains may often be done with a counselor, trusted friend, or prayer partner. Talking out the hurt, asking God to heal it, and forgiving the person for specific hurts pours balm on the wound. This can take time. This can be especially helpful when we have no idea how to begin or where to start. Trusted friends can also offer a neutral perspective, can help ferret out your feelings, and can push or support you when needed.

Write it Out: Alternatively, journaling or writing prayers can also offer the opportunity for healing and forgiving. Writing is a great way to get started because we are not restricted by time or coherent thought. We can begin with a stream of consciousness and then move into specifics. *Appendix A* includes journal prompts and blank and lined journal pages to reproduce for your personal use.

Appendix B is a worksheet to help you think through the hurts you have experienced and process some of the underlying pain. It is only one of many ways to begin questioning yourself and writing, speaking, or praying about the things you need to forgive. Maybe you will start and then stop and come back to it a few days later. These things take time. Permit yourself to let it take time. The Spirit will work in that time, and your heart will change. If there are numerous incidents with one person you want to process, consider each one in due time. There is no need to rush through this exercise. Instead, be specific in naming the hurt and the forgiveness.

Find the Truth: There are many hurts and many situations that may require forgiveness. But the pain *can* be healed. God has given us many promises of His healing in the Bible. Take time to look up the promises of God throughout Scripture. *Appendix C* has a list of verses related to forgiveness to help you get started.

Consider also what God may have to say about the specific pain and feelings you have when considering past incidents. Many verses speak to our hurts. Take time to look them up and maybe even write them down or memorize them. This, too, will be a soothing balm on your wounds. For example, in one of the previous chapters, I talked about how I felt left out and not good enough. The truth that I can apply to that pain of "not enough" is that I am His "handiwork, created in Christ Jesus to do good works, which God prepared in advance for [me] to do" (Eph. 2:10). I am a branch of Jesus Christ and cared for by the Vinedresser (John 15:1, 5). The Lord is mighty who saves and rejoices over me (Zeph. 3:17). He rejoices over me!

The Bible also offers a balm in the truths of God and who He is. When we struggle with forgiveness, it can be refreshing to see that God is unchanging and faithful. He has cast our sins to the depths of the sea (Micah 7:19). When we despair over the friend or family member who doesn't change, we can find hope and comfort in knowing nothing is impossible with God (Luke 18:27).

Either way, when writing, praying, or talking, the Spirit will move in and through the words. He will reveal your heart and pain, and He will comfort and soothe the hurt, healing you from the inside. The Spirit may also reveal things that you had forgotten but are essential in understanding the offender or the pain.

Memories: Reclaiming Enemy Territory

Is there anything easy about forgiveness? Forgiving others, forgiving ourselves, and healing all take work—especially when our memory continues to bring up past decisions, choices, actions, and reactions. In chapter four, we looked at David and Bathsheba as an example of regret. Let's consider them again. There was some serious sin and hurt going on in that relationship. David did not consider his sin for months, so I guess he had no disturbing thoughts or memories of the events. Was Bathsheba the same? Or perhaps Bathsheba fondly recalled her husband and hated David for having him killed? Did she remember her betrayal every time she saw David or her growing belly? Did she hold the pain tight, or did it come back at strange times in the night?

Whatever our torment is, why do we keep thinking of it? Why does it keep coming to mind? Our minds, our memories, and the enemy will dredge it back up and remind us of all the emotion behind it—the anger, the sorrow, the desire for revenge, the pull of depression and isolation, the hopelessness or guilt or whatever the feeling is that comes. *None of that is from God.*

When David looked at Bathsheba, for a time, he must have remembered how he had come to marry her. Did he think, "I am an adulterer, a murderer, and wife stealer?" Did he think about never approaching Bathsheba again and just making sure that she was comfortable and taken care of? After all, then he wouldn't have to be reminded of those sins. These are the thoughts that come to us in the darkness. Avoidance and guilt and sorrow. But none of those are from God because we have been given a Spirit of "power, love, and self-discipline" (2 Tim. 1:7). But once forgiven, we need to reclaim the battlefield of our minds. We have to call out to God to defeat the thoughts that trap us in the past and the arrows of the enemy. Remember, He walks with us as we address the consequences of sin and live with a change of heart.

Call it Out to Defeat It

When we are reminded of our past transgressions or those of others who have hurt us, we need to declare the truth of God by recognizing the work of Christ in our lives and the lives of others. The work that He has already completed and is continuing to do. We must call out the emotions that pull us down and trap us again in that web.

State the truth of forgiveness and the situation. We need not ask for forgiveness again. Doing so is like continuing to make payments on a house that is already paid in full. There is no account upon which to credit another payment to the mortgage company. We are forgiven. State this truth: "I am already forgiven, and my sin is taken away." Say it out loud; declare it. State it now for the offender. Say: "{Insert name here} is forgiven. God has taken their offense from me. I walk in His light and life, not the shadow of this person and what they have done." We have to declare the truth of the situation in light of God and His intervention.

No matter the memories that creep in and tell us lies, we can confidently say: "I am forgiven, and I have forgiven. God has forgiven me and loves me. God has chosen me as His own, His daughter. God is my comfort and my joy."

Talk about the consequences. Talk to God and to those who are affected by the consequences. After their baby died, David went to Bathsheba and comforted her. How often do we avoid people who have been involved in our issues? We just want to forget and hope they do too. But David spent time with his wife and made new memories. I think that is key to living through the consequences. Avoidance adds anxiety to our situation, whereas accepting the consequences and living through them aids the change process.

Can you think of how the prodigal son would have responded if he didn't interact with those most hurt by his choices? In that case, he would have declined to attend the banquet that his father wanted to throw for him. It would be quite a different story. We would have a gloating brother who says, "Hmmm, he got his due," rather than a story of mercy and grace. Both David and the prodigal—after having met with the Father—modeled working through the consequences by interacting with those they had hurt. Mercy and grace are part of this whole process as we work through it all with God and others.

Worship and have a change of heart. In the last chapter, we looked at how David worshiped God and went forth with a changed heart. These are the actions that are part of our everyday worship. We are called to offer ourselves as a "living sacrifice" in worship to God and to be transformed by the "renewing of our minds" (Rom. 12:1-2). This kind of worship that we are called to is putting God at the center of our lives, whereas the sin put ourselves or others in our focal point. Adoring God reminds us that He knows better and does better than we can ever imagine. Worship places us in His arms again, malleable to His will and His changes. This worship is our lives, but it is also a specific time set aside to focus on God and declare His praises. Worship Him and give Him room to renew you.

These are the things that happen in this amazing experience of forgiveness and turning to God. His walking beside us, with us, and in us daily as we sin and suffer consequences and recover and become more like Jesus—this is the life of a Christian. Forgiveness is just part of it. A hard part, but the person we are becoming is worth it.

Reflection

1. Take time in prayer to identify how you best process thoughts and feelings. Is it writing? Talking? Consider who you may approach to discuss these issues.

2. Take time to write out some of the truths that help you stand firm in forgiveness.

CHAPTER 6
UNLIKELY RECONCILIATION

So, we have looked at forgiveness, unforgiveness, indications of a lack of forgiveness, and I think that the most pressing thing to consider now is the relationships that are post-forgiveness. Yes . . . that would mean reconciliation (I guess you knew that from the title of this chapter, no way around that). You may be asking, "Do I have to reconcile? Do I want to reconcile?"

Forgiveness is all about recognizing, confessing, and repenting of sin so that we will heal. Sometimes relationships heal too, but it does take work. And sometimes relationships are not healed; they are suffered through or severed. Relationships take two people. Sometimes more in the case of family or group pains. But we will focus on two parties knowing that it could be several. Two people work together to make a relationship, and relationships are based on trust. Sin breaks that trust. It is the rebuilding of trust in a relationship that constitutes reconciliation.

Sin and Repentance in Relationships

So, first, we will consider the sin in the relationship. I hadn't considered the story in Matthew 18 to be related to forgiveness and reconciliation until just recently. This is the section of Matthew often titled "Dealing with Sin in the Church." Remember these verses: talk to just that person about their sin, and then more people, and more if they "refuse to listen." This "refuse to listen" is quite clearly speaking to repentance. What Jesus is saying to us is that when sin is brought to light within a relationship, there is opportunity for forgiveness, change, repentance, and reconciliation. A clear point is made: "If they refuse to listen even to the church, treat them as you would a pagan or a tax collector" (Matt. 18:17). Treating the offender as a pagan or tax collector is the equivalent of "have nothing more to do with them."

Reconciliation does not always have to be the end goal in forgiveness. That is what these few lines say here in Matthew 18. We forgive the offender, but in this case, the offender does not have a change of heart and is set out from fellowship. Paul also gives us an example. In 2 Timothy 4:14-15, Paul says that the Lord will repay Alexander for what he has done and warns others away from the metalworker. This may indicate forgiveness since Paul trusts that God will handle the punishment, but it doesn't sound like any reconciliation took place. In verse 16, Paul speaks of others who harmed him, but again he indicates forgiveness that does not include reconciliation.

So, in some way, the pressure is off. We do not *have* to reconcile, provided that the person has not repented. So, if they do not repent, we can cut them out. What a relief, right!? Well, even if it is acceptable, I think in that case, we miss out on an opportunity for growth in Christ. We also recognize the reality of life is that we do not always have the luxury of cutting people out of our lives. They remain a colleague, fellow church member, family member, or ex-family member. We inevitably see these people and continue to interact with them.

Even though we may have Jesus' "permission" to walk away, we are still called to forgive and to continue healing through continued interactions with the offender. The relationship will inevitably *change* because of their lack of repentance and also because of your act of forgiveness and steps toward healing. Our healing will make the new relationship bearable and maybe even joyful. After all, God is with us and in us, even in those interactions.

Our healing will make the new relationship bearable and maybe even joyful.

Persevering in Broken Relationships

It isn't always practical to cut people out of our lives after relationships are broken. We live in a broken world and with broken people, so we also find ourselves in broken relationships with people. So, how do we go forward with these broken relationships?

Forgiveness Above All

Forgiveness is the only way to break the chains that bind us to the hurt that a person has inflicted on us. With that loosing of chains, followed by healing, we will be more prepared to handle broken relationships. At this point in the book, there is little more to add!

Prayer Next

Matthew 5:44 says, "Pray for those who persecute you." Prayers are going to be our BFF (Best Friend Forever) when dealing with broken relationships. Praying for enemies is a command from Jesus, and it may well start as a rote activity, but the Holy Spirit will use it also to change us and conform us more to Jesus. Praying for the other person is not just about punishment or justice for the offenses. It is about God working in them, blessing them, changing their heart, and praying for that person to succeed. Prayers of gratitude for our enemies will heap coals on their heads and shield us from additional pain. These are not easy prayers, but they are necessary prayers. They are part of the commands that we are given for our own good.

Prayers for our enemies will also change us, but so will prayers for ourselves in handling the encounters. Prayers for ourselves—asking for patience and peace in dealing with former offenders (especially unreformed offenders)—will also be our companion. Prayers to be a blessing and the salt and light to people in these interactions will be answered, for we know they are God's will. The old hurts are easily brought back to the surface, and we will likely have those silent cries to God "Help me, Lord!" By praying in advance, we can prepare our hearts and allow the Spirit to act and not ourselves.

Wear the Armor of God

Interacting with those who have hurt us and are unwilling to change is hard. We need the armor of God (Eph. 6:10-18). We need to stand firm in truth, righteousness, and the gospel. We need to stand firm in our faith in God and in our salvation as we let the Spirit of God work and move through us. We need to know the truth of our position as a child of God and what that means for us. We need to know deep within that we have been made righteous, and we are forgiven for our part in the relationship that is broken. We need to know the gospel and be rooted in the Word of God to withstand all attacks in the coming interactions of brokenness.

The depth of our pain is generally an indicator of our need to seek truth as we push on in broken relationships. Seek specific verses to recall for the person and your interactions with them. If you feel unloved and forgotten when in the same room with this person, seek verses that speak God's truth into your life: He is the God who sees me (Gen. 16:13), and God loves me (1 John 4:16).

We need constancy in our faith and unwavering belief in our salvation. The enemy (the offender and Satan's army) will try in every way to attack in interactions we are forced to continue with instead of cutting off. The Holy Spirit must be our companion to guide us and lift us from these difficult interactions. The Spirit is our only offensive weapon in the armor, so let the Spirit work in the person and the relationship; invite that work.

Love your Enemies

I referenced Matthew 5:44 up there regarding prayer but left out the first part of that verse: Love your enemies. Yes, another command. We do have to love our enemies. We have to be the example of God's love in these broken relationships. "Let us not become weary in doing good, for at the proper time we will reap a harvest if we do not give up" (Gal. 6:9). It will be a wearying thing to continue contact with those whom we feel we are better off without. But God will fill us with the strength to do so and will walk with us in this quest to never weary in doing good to our enemies, this quest to love our enemies.

Love is an action, a choice, so how exactly to love our enemies is a broad question. It is difficult to say because we don't have cookie-cutter relationships. It is a choice. It is likely a choice to evaluate on a moment-by-moment basis. Since love is action-able, we have to start with action, and the heart will follow. Consider how you would act if this were a different person, maybe someone you like and respect. Then act as if it were that person. If you would treat the person you respect with love, then act in love in the broken relationship. Most of these fall under respectful treatment. Greet them; treat them well. Compliment them—even to other people or in front of others. Turn your other cheek if they do offend you. Respond in ways that reflect the Jesus who lives in you and walks with you.

Hope in the Lord

In Romans 8, Paul speaks first of our suffering and then our victory in Christ. When we walk in these broken relationships in a broken world, these victorious words can be the ones that lend us hope. First, the Spirit of God—the power of God in us—helps us in our weakness (Rom. 8:26). And second, "in all these things we are more than conquerors through him who loved us" (Rom. 8:37). With God in us and for us, we endure in these difficult, challenging, sometimes heart-breaking relations. Through forgiveness, prayer, and girding ourselves with the armor of God, we will be much better equipped to love our enemies and persevere in our broken relationships.

Reflection

1. Write out a prayer for the person who wronged you—specifically for this person. Pray this prayer daily to bless them.

2. Look up Ephesians 6:10-18 and study in-depth the armor of God. Consider how each piece puts your heart and mind in the right place with God.

3. Love is action. What small steps can you take to act out God's love for the person who wronged you?

CHAPTER 7
BIBLICAL RECONCILIATION

Though Matthew 18 seems to give us a "way out," I fully believe that God wants us to reconcile. It was the ultimate example for God to send His own Son to reconcile us to Him, and He has given us the ministry of reconciliation as well—to help others reconcile to Him (2 Cor. 5:18). If that's the case, I think reconciliation in our relationships is a healthy goal. In the illustration in Matthew 18:15-20, the brother who sins against us is given no fewer than three chances to consider their sin. There is an ache in the lack of reconciliation because we were made to love, and we were made for fellowship.

We were made for loving fellowship, which includes forgiveness *and* reconciliation. In most relationships, it is ongoing: we arrive late, we apologize; we push on issues, offend, and apologize. The relationship goes on despite the hurts that also go on because we're two sinners in a broken world trying to live out the gospel of love. Many of our relationships grow and develop over time during this cycle. Others deteriorate or morph into something else.

When we want to reconcile after hurt, I think there is great hope for the relationship. There are several reconciliation stories in the Bible we can look at: Esau and Jacob, Paul and Mark, etc. The one that I feel most compelled to look at is Joseph's reconciliation with his brothers. In this story, we can see how Joseph maturely addressed the reconciliation through an honest account of his feelings and by testing others' change of heart in the slow rebuilding of trust.

We were made for loving fellowship, which includes forgiveness and reconciliation.

Process of Reconciling

The story of Joseph's reconciliation is long, stretching from Genesis 42 to 50. I think it is fitting that this story of reconciliation takes so many pages to tell and falls so close to the beginning of our human history. Reconciliation is a process, and the story being told in such detail and falling so early in the Bible seems to underscore the importance. Most of what we will look at is in chapters 42 to 45 if you want to read it again and look at the nuances.

Reluctant to Engage

Joseph was skeptical of his brothers, even calling them spies who had come to plot out ways to steal grain needed during the drought. We, too, do not have to go into reconciliation with our hearts on our sleeves. It is normal to fear additional hurt from people who have hurt us in the past. What is not healthy is to allow the fear of hurt to keep us from engaging and moving a relationship forward. Again, we are not given a Spirit of fear (2 Tim. 1:7). God's perfect love drives out fear (1 John 4:18). So, we focus on God's love and move forward in love to reach the former offender.

Test the Change of Heart

Joseph heard the evidence of heart change in his brothers' conversation of regret. They spoke of what they did to him so many years ago and that they must pay for their mistakes. So, Joseph had an idea that these brothers may have changed; they at least had noted in their hearts that they had done wrong. Was there a change of heart? Had they really repented? To find out, he tested them.

> Test 1: He tested them by keeping one brother in exchange for bringing the last brother to prove they were not spies. I'm sure he wondered what they would do; after all, he was left for dead. Would they do the same to this brother?
>
> Test 2: On top of keeping one brother, he also gave them back the silver used as payment for the grain they came to buy. Would they be honest and return it? Did they have a changed heart?

These two tests happen simultaneously. Joseph was pushing to find out if his brothers had a true change of heart. But then he waited. He must have waited months because the food was gone by the time the brothers returned to purchase more. How did the brothers measure up to Joseph's testing?

Test Answer 1: The brothers finally returned, and they

did bring the youngest, Joseph's brother Benjamin. They did not leave their brother for dead.

Test Answer 2: They also immediately disclosed that they found the silver payment in their sacks of grain the last time. Immediate disclosure of an issue is a definite sign of a change of heart.

So, the brothers did not behave as they had in the past, leaving one brother for dead; they had not harmed their other half-brother. They *had* changed.

They also passed the second test. They noticed something that would be a block to trust, and they disclosed it even before meeting with Joseph (Gen. 43:19-23). They knew they could be punished for what had happened or turned away and sent back to watch their families starve. Instead, they discussed the issue and asked for mercy. More evidence of change.

But Joseph wasn't ready to put himself out there yet; he still didn't tell his brothers who he was. He needed to give it more time. I would like to think that Joseph was praying for them all and for the relationship at this time. Still, he set them to another test.

Test 3: Joseph secretly had a silver cup put into Benjamin's bag before the brothers left and sent one of his men after them to find out where it had gone. Now Joseph would know if the brothers were going to take care of their half-brother, too.

Test Answer 3: The brothers were terrified at what would happen to Benjamin, and immediately went back to face the issue and submitted themselves to Joseph. Judah even insisted on taking Benjamin's place and submitted himself for punishment.

It took three tests and quite a bit of time passing before Joseph was ready to reveal himself to his brothers.

Joseph Models Reconciliation

I think that we can take this story as a model of the reconciliation process. It is a natural protective instinct to hesitate to engage with those who have hurt us in the past. Joseph tested the change of heart that he hoped for in his brothers. But he didn't tell them what he was doing, and that is the one thing that I think we can do differently—we can talk about our hope for reconciliation with the offender. At the death of their father, the brothers worried that Joseph still held a grudge against them and therefore contrived to say that Jacob called upon Joseph to forgive them; they even threw themselves upon him, saying they would be his slaves. Because of Joseph's secrecy, the brothers feared his true intentions. Maturing relationships should strive to be open, discussing the tests and the hesitation of hurting in reconciliation. This kind of openness would have assured the brothers of Joseph's true feelings toward them. Remember, it is what has been brought to light that is of God—the things that remain in darkness are what hold us back and bring us down. So, maybe Joseph isn't an ideal reconciliation story, but a model starting place for sure. He took his time, tested the change of heart, and didn't let fear rule over the relationship.

Reconciliation is possible with time and patience. We are fallible humans who need grace in relationships. Openly discussing the process and how we feel as we seek to reconcile is the best way to ensure that both parties are enabled to make the reconciliation succeed.

Putting it All Together

Let us return now to the two brothers that opened our discussion of forgiveness—the parable of the prodigal son. It is too bad that the story does not continue, exploring the relationship between the two brothers. But I think this is the case because our primary relationship—the one we have to "get right"—is the one with God. Remember that the Father was always looking for the prodigal to return home. Remember that the Father sought out the older son to invite him into the fullness he was offering.

We have a choice to make: to follow God or to follow self. I have often focused on what was being taken away—a whole season of life stolen by my anger and disappointment. I was thinking of the things that I had wanted, "if only." Even when I do not sense an abundant life, I need only lay claim to it. I can have life "beyond what is expected," for that is what *abundant* means.

You see, the father came to each of the sons with an offer, and our Father has approached us as well. He sent His Son to reconcile us to Him. Once our relationship is right with Him, and we understand His character—who He truly is—then we live beyond our expectations. We find that because He is faithful, we are able to let go of the pain. Because revenge is His, we are able to let go of the need for it ourselves. Because He is loving, we are able to receive His forgiveness. We know that He will care for us and take care of our enemies. We believe in Him. Accept His love and forgiveness and believe. Then we can come alive again in Him and live abundantly.

In the strength of this belief, then we can take steps to heal the pains of the past, forgive others, and reconcile relationships. He has called us to Him so that we may live abundant lives. Abundant lives are not characterized by the flags of unforgiveness or the bitterness of the past. Abundant lives are characterized by forgiveness, compassion, love, kindness, and peace. Abundant lives are full of joy and the Spirit and all of His fruits.

So, please take up the challenge to forgive and make the steps necessary to heal. Meditate on His word. Know Him personally through the Word and prayer. Seek others who can help you process pain and journal out your feelings with the leading of the Spirit. Find healing in forgiveness.

Reflection

1. Have you persisted in a relationship that needs trust to be rebuilt? Pray for the person or people involved and bring it to the light. Seek to begin the process by talking it out.

2. Take time to identify the most difficult part of the healing process for you personally. Take it to the Lord in faith that He will give you strength to push through the hard parts into the abundant life He desires for you!

ACKNOWLEDGMENTS

This book has been a labor over the past year. I have learned and processed much in the writing and pray that you will receive as much reading and working through forgiveness.

Thank you to my Lord and Savior Jesus Christ for His redeeming work and guidance in writing this.

Thank you to my family and friends, and especially my husband, who have supported and encouraged me in this writing endeavor.

Thank you, readers, for persevering to forgive those who have hurt you and choosing this resource to walk with you. If you liked this book, please check out my site, https://www.inspiritencourage.com, for more Christian encouragement. I love to hear from readers, so please reach out.

Was this book helpful? Did you get something from it? Please visit Amazon or Goodreads and leave a review of this book. Every review makes this book more visible to others. https://www.amazon.com/review/create-review?asin=B096K98L11

To join our advance reader group, sign up here https://www.subscribepage.com/flamingdovearc

Christian Books in Multiple Genres, Join Christian Indie Author ~ Readers Group on Facebook. Opportunities to learn more great Christian authors. https://www.facebook.com/groups/291215317668431/

APPENDIX A

JOURNAL PROMPTS

Lord, help me today as I struggle to forgive . . .

Lord, I don't know how to forgive, but I want to . . .

Jesus, You said that we are to forgive even 77 times. Show me ...

Lord, I keep thinking of when I ...

Jesus, thank You for Your sacrifice on the cross, forgiving me for . . .

Jesus, I'm sorry I have . . .

Lord, I need Your healing touch . . .

Father God, I hurt over what happened when . . .

I need Your help to get through this Lord . . .

I need Your joy to be my strength because today I do not have . . .

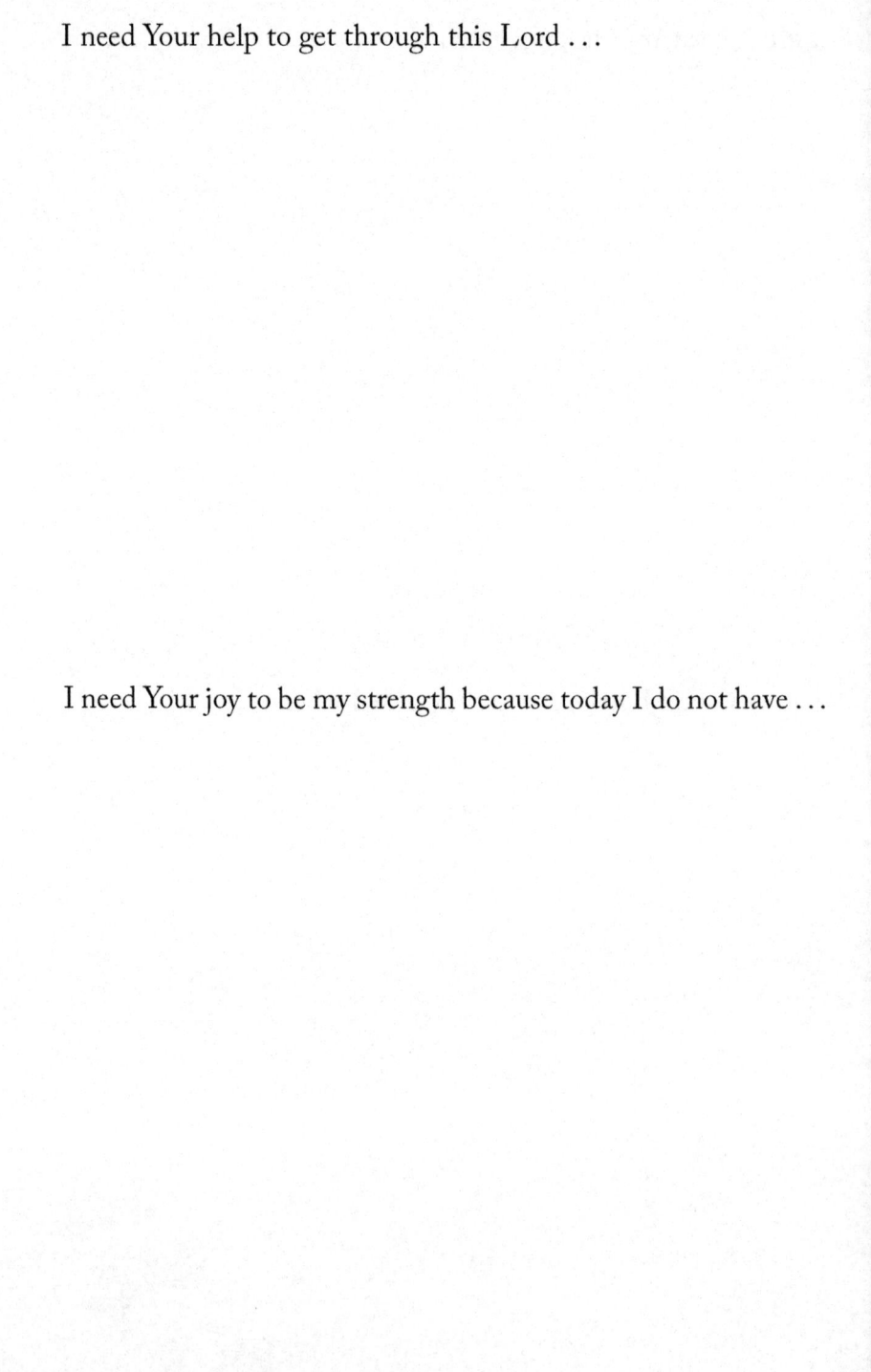

Lord, Your love is overwhelming . . .

Come Holy Spirit and work in . . .

Change my heart, oh God . . .

Father, shine Your lamp upon . . .

Lord, I lift my eyes to the hills, seeking Your help . . .

APPENDIX B

HEALING IN FORGIVENESS WORKSHEET

Who was involved in the incident?

Describe the incident(s). Be specific.

What do you feel when you think on this?

What does God say about the incident?

What does God say to you about the incident?

How has God shown His hand in this incident?

What do I want God to do for me about this incident and the feelings I have?

What do I want God to do for the offender?

APPENDIX C

If we confess our sins, he is faithful and just and will forgive us our sins and purify us from all unrighteousness.

1 John 1:9

Whoever would foster love covers over an offense, but whoever repeats the matter separates close friends.

Proverbs 17:9

Therefore, if anyone is in Christ, the new creation has come: The old has gone, the new is here!

2 Corinthians 5:17

But I tell you that everyone will have to give account on the day of judgment for every empty word they have spoken.

Matthew 12:36

For the Spirit God gave us does not make us timid, but gives us power, love and self-discipline.

2 Timothy 1:7

Blessed are the merciful, for they will be shown mercy.
Matthew 5:7

But you are a chosen people, a royal priesthood, a holy nation, God's special possession, that you may declare the praises of him who called you out of darkness into his wonderful light.
1 Peter 2:9

Peacemakers who sow in peace reap a harvest of righteousness.
James 3:18

A new command I give you: Love one another. As I have loved you, so you must love one another. John 13:34

But if a wicked person turns away from the wickedness they have committed and does what is just and right, they will save their life. Ezekiel 18:27

Blessed are those who hunger and thirst for righteousness, for they will be filled. Matthew 5:6

Therefore, as God's chosen people, holy and dearly loved, clothe yourselves with compassion, kindness, humility, gentleness and patience. Bear with each other and forgive one another if any of you has a grievance against someone. Forgive as the Lord forgave you. And over all these virtues put on love, which binds them all together in perfect unity. Colossians 3:12-14

Get rid of all bitterness, rage and anger, brawling and slander, along with every form of malice.
Be kind and compassionate to one another,
forgiving each other, just as in Christ God forgave you.
Ephesians 4:31-32

If I speak in the tongues of men or of angels, but do not have love, I am only a resounding gong or a clanging cymbal.
1 Corinthians 13:1

But you are a chosen people, a royal priesthood, a holy nation, God's special possession, that you may declare the praises of him who called you out of darkness into his wonderful light.
1 Peter 2:9

Gracious words are a honeycomb,
sweet to the soul and healing to the bones. Proverbs 16:24

Do not conform to the pattern of this world, but be transformed by the renewing of your mind. Then you will be able to test and approve what God's will is—his good, pleasing and perfect will. Romans 12:2

The Lord is my shepherd, I lack nothing. He makes me lie down in green pastures, he leads me beside quiet waters, he refreshes my soul. He guides me along the right paths for his name's sake. Even though I walk through the darkest valley, I will fear no evil, for you are with me; your rod and your staff, they comfort me. Psalm 23:1-4

I lift up my eyes to the mountains—where does my help come from? My help comes from the Lord,
the Maker of heaven and earth. Psalm 121:1-2

Do not take revenge, my dear friends, but leave room for God's wrath, for it is written: "It is mine to avenge; I will repay," says the Lord. On the contrary: If your enemy is hungry, feed him; if he is thirsty, give him something to drink. In doing this you will heap burning coals on his head.

Do not be overcome by evil, but overcome evil with good.
Matthew 12:19-21

~*~

Make every effort to live in peace with everyone and to be holy; without holiness no one will see the Lord. Hebrews 12:14

~*~

But blessed is the one who trusts in the Lord, whose confidence is in him. They will be like a tree planted by the water that sends out its roots by the stream. It does not fear when heat comes; its leaves are always green. It has no worries in a year of drought and never fails to bear fruit. Jeremiah 17:7-8

~*~

Therefore, since we are surrounded by such a great cloud of witnesses, let us throw off everything that hinders and the sin that so easily entangles. And let us run with perseverance the race marked out for us, fixing our eyes on Jesus, the pioneer and perfecter of faith. For the joy set before him he endured the cross, scorning its shame, and sat down at the right hand of the throne of God. Hebrews 12:1-2

~*~

Peace I leave with you; my peace I give you. I do not give to you as the world gives. Do not let your hearts be troubled and do not be afraid. John 14:27

~*~

FORGIVEN Psalm 103:11-12

Consider looking up verses or stories from the Bible that address your needs. Topics to search:

Anger	Healing
Hurt	Strength
Broken heart	Identity
Reconciliation	Guilt
Change	Peace
Suffering	Hope

ABOUT THE AUTHOR

Author and speaker Sarah K Howley was born and raised in Texas together with three siblings. She obtained a Bachelor of Arts in Speech Communication from Texas A&M University. Upon graduation, she worked in marketing and then moved into teaching. She then returned to school for a Master of Education in Curriculum & Instruction at the University of Houston. She has taught all ages, from elementary to adult. While living in Italy, she obtained a certificate in Christian counseling.

Sarah has lived in America, Europe, Africa, and Asia, and met her husband in Italy, though he too is from the United States. She writes a blog at inspiritencourage.com and accompanies her husband around the world for his job. She writes because she wants to encourage others to "grab on to biblical truths to walk in faith.

ENDNOTES

1   "Forgiveness: Defined," Greater Good Magazine, accessed January 23, 2020, https://greatergood.berkeley.edu/topic/forgiveness/definition.

2   "Forgiveness," Wikipedia, accessed January 23, 2020, https://en.wikipedia.org/wiki/Forgiveness.

3   "5 Astonishing Real Examples of Forgiveness,"beliefnet.com, accessed April 21, 2020, https://www.beliefnet.com/faiths/christianity/galleries/5-astonishing-real-examples-of-forgiveness.aspx. See also: https://www.today.com/news/how-do-you-forgive-killer-mother-moves-past-tragedy-4B11203330

4   Beth Moore, Chasing Vines: Finding Your Way to an Immensely Fruitful Life (Carol Stream, IL: Tyndale House Publishers, 2020), 169.

Printed in Great Britain
by Amazon